Wit & Humour

FELIX BENTLEY

Published by Bradwell Books
9 Orgreave Close Sheffield S13 9NP
Email: books@bradwellbooks.co.uk
Compiled by Felix Bentley

British Library Cataloguing in Publication Data: a catalogue record for this book is available from the British Library.

1st Edition

ISBN: 9781909914506

Print: Gomer Press, Llandysul, Ceredigion SA44 4JL
Design by: jenksdesign@yahoo.co.uk/07506 471162

At a primary school in Tarporley the teacher came up with a good problem for her maths class to solve.

"Suppose, there were a dozen sheep and six of them jumped over a fence," she said to the group of seven-year-olds, "How many would be left?"

Little Harry, a farmer's son, put his hand up. "Nowt," he answered.

"None?" exclaimed his teacher. "Harry, I'm afraid you don't know your arithmetic."

"Really, Miss?" said Harry, cockily, "And you don't know your sheep. When one goes, they all go!"

A man walks into a pub in Macclesfield with a Chester pork pie on his head.

The barman asks, "Ah do, youth, why are you wearing a Chester pork pie on yer head?"

The man replies, "It's a family tradition. We always wear Chester pork pies on our heads on Tuesday."

The barman says, "But it's Wednesday."

Sheepishly, the man says, "Man, I must look like a real fool."

A gang of robbers broke into the Chester Lawyers' Club by mistake. The old legal lions put up a fierce fight for their lives and their money. The gang was happy to escape in one piece. "It ain't so bad," one crook said. "At least we got fifty quid between us."

His boss screamed at him, "I warned you to stay clear of lawyers... we had 200 quid when we broke in!"

Q: What do you call a cat that lives in an igloo?
A: An eskimew!

At a cricket match in Alderley Edge a fast bowler sent one down and it just clipped the bail. As nobody yelled "Ow's att", the batsman picked up the bail and replaced it. He looked at the umpire and said, "Windy today, int it?"

"Yes," said the umpire, "Mind it doesn't blow your cap off when you're walking back to the pavilion."

Many years ago, a miner fell down shaft in the Bredbury Pits. The deputy shouted,"Have you broken anything, youth?"

"No," called back the miner,"There's not much to break down here!"

Insurance Assessor: "What gear were you in at the moment of the impact?"

Woman Driver:"Gucci sweats and Reeboks."

A Cheshire man is driving through Staffordshire, when he passes a farmer standing in the middle of a huge field. He pulls the car over and watches the farmer standing stock-still, doing absolutely nothing. Intrigued, the man walks over to the farmer and asks him, "Excuse me sir, but what are you doing?"

The farmer replies, "I'm trying to win a Nobel Prize."
"How?" Asks the puzzled Cheshire man.

"Well," says the farmer, "I heard they give the prize to people who are outstanding in their field."

The owner of a large company in Chester went down to check out how everything was going. He notices a young man just relaxing with his feet up in the coffee room. "Just how much are you getting paid a week?" asked the guvnor.

"Two hundred quid!" Replies the young man.

Taking out his wallet, the boss hands him two hundred pounds and says, "Here is a week's pay. Now don't come back!" A supervisor walks, in with a piece of paper, just as the young man goes out the door. The boss asks him, "How long was that lazy git working here?"

"He doesn't work here," says the supervisor, "He was just waiting for me to give him these directions!"

Two aerials meet on a roof, fall in love, get married. The ceremony was rubbish - but the reception was brilliant.

Why couldn't the lifeguard save the hippie?

He was too far out, man!

A man went to the doctor one day and said, "I've just been playing rugby for the Widnes Vikings. and when I got back, I found that when I touched my legs, my arms, my head, and everywhere else, it really hurt."

After careful examination the doctor concluded, "I'm afraid you've broken your finger."

One day a rich man from Knutsford was driving his Mercedes Benz past a field near Kelsall and he saw a shabby man standing there chewing grass. The rich man stopped the car and asked the man, "Why are you eating grass"

The man replied, "I am very, very poor and hungry and I have no money to buy food."

The rich man tells him to climb in the car, "Come home with me to Knutsford."

The poor man shakes his head and says, "But I can't. I have six children out in this field, all eating grass too."

The rich man says,"That doesn't matter, they're all welcome to come home with me to eat."

So the poor man rounds up his kids and they all get in the Mercedes. The poor man can't thank the rich man enough, "I'm so very grateful, sir."

"That's okay," says the rich man,"You should see the grass in my garden, it must be a foot high."

A passenger in a taxi tapped the driver on the shoulder to ask him something. The driver screamed, lost control of the cab, nearly hit a bus, drove up over the curb and stopped just inches from a large plate glass window.

For a few moments everything was silent in the cab, then the driver said, "Please, don't ever do that again. You scared the daylights out of me."

The passenger, who was also frightened, apologised and said he didn'trealise that a tap on the shoulder could frighten him so much, to which thedriver replied, "I'm sorry, it's really not your fault at all. Today is myfirst day driving a cab. I've been driving a hearse for the last twenty-five years."

A group of backpackers from Chester University were sitting around a campfire one evening when a stranger asked to join them. Glad to add to their group, they agreed. The evening's fun soon turned to jokes. One of the students started to tell jokes in which Keele University was the butt of the humour. The stranger who, it turned out, had graduated from Keele University himself, became more and more furious with each quip. Finally, he had had enough and pulled out his razor and began to threaten the Chester lads with it. Fortunately for them, he couldn't find a socket to plug it into.

Supporters, waiting to watch Crewe Alexandra play Port Vale, heard that the Port Vale players were going to be delayed.

They saw a sign on the M6 that said "Clean Lavatories"... so they did.

Crewe Alexandra beat Port Vale five – nothing; they were lucky to get nothing.

A plain Jane from Prestbury goes to see Madame Grizelda, a fortune-teller, and asks about her future love life.

Madame Grizelda tells her, "Two men are madly in love with you – Mark and Maurice."

"Who will be the lucky one?" asks Jane excitedly.

Madame Grizelda answers, "Maurice will marry you, and Mark will be the lucky one."

"You're looking glum," the captain of Boughton Hall C.C. remarked to one of his players.

"Yes, the doctor says I can't play cricket," said the downcast man.

"Really?" replied the captain, "I didn't know he'd ever seen you play?"

A lad from Widnes who had just started his first term at Keele University asked a third year, "Can you tell me where the library's at?"

The older student said disdainfully, "At Keele University, we never end a sentence with a preposition."

The new boy tried again, "Can you tell me where the library's at, you lanky lummock?"

A man from Wilmslow decided to become a monk so he went to the monastery and talked to the head monk.

The head monk said, "You must take a vow of silence and can only say two words every three years."

The man agreed and after the first three years, the head monk came to him and said, "What are your two words?"

"Food cold!" the man replied.

Three more years went by and the head monk came to him and said, "What are your two words?"

"Robe dirty!" the man exclaimed.

Three more years went by and the head monk came to him and said, "What are your two words?"

"I quit!" said the man.

"Well," the head monk replied, "I'm not surprised. You've done nothing but complain ever since you got here!"

A Warrington man fell out with his in-laws and banned them from entering the house while he was in it. His wife faithfully carried out his wishes until she was on her death bed and then asked sadly, "Haven't I always been a supportive wife to you, John?"

"Yes, me duck," he replied, "The best."

"Then I would love it if you could grant my last request and let my sister Sarah ride in the first car with you at my funeral?"

"Alright, my duck," he agreed heavily, "But I'm warning you, it'll spoil all me pleasure!"

Two blokes are standing in the Nantwich Job Centre, waiting for their turn at the counter.

The first bloke says to the second one,"I have to buy my wife something nice for our wedding anniversary and the benefits cheque won't cover it."

The second bloke looks up from his paper and says,"What date?"

The first bloke thinks for a while and says,"15th September."
The second bloke considers his next question."What year?"
Without taking a breath, the first bloke replies,"Every year for the last twenty-seven!

Two council workers on a site in Chester are surveying land they're about to dig up.

The gaffer says to one of them, "You go and get the metal detector and check for pipe work and I'll get the kettle on and have a brew."

The gaffer gets the tea going while his mate starts work. Half-hour later the gaffer puts his paper down, next to his mug of tea, to find out how work is progressing and he finds his mate sitting on a wall scratching his head.

"What's up with you?" The gaffer asks. "There's pipework all over the place. Look!"

The young worker sets off across the land, the bleeper sounding continuously as the detector passes in front of him. The gaffer watches him, laughing, then he says, "Are you soft or what? You're wearing steel toe caps in your boots!"

Down the King's Head, a group of blokes sit around drinking when a mobile phone on the table rings. One of the men picks up the mobile and puts the speaker-phone on.

A woman's voice says, "How are you, darling? I hope you don't mind but I've just seen a diamond ring priced £2000 and wondered if I can buy it? I've got your credit card with me."

"Of course, my dear, go ahead," answers the man.

"While I'm on," purrs the lady, "I've noticed a top of the range car I'd like. It's only £65,000, could I order that as well?"

"Of course, my angel," replies the man.

His friends around the table look at each other in disbelief as the lady continues, "And I've just noticed a house in Alderley Edge, lover. It's only £750,000 - could we have that as well please?"

"Of course, sugar," answers the man, without so much as blinking.

The phone call is ended and the man smiles at the others and takes a long swill of beer. Then he looks around and shouts "Anyone know whose phone this is?"

It was match day for Crewe Alexandra and excited crowds filled the streets, heading for Gresty Road. A funeral procession drove slowly through the throng. One of the Crewe supporters stopped, took off his hat and bowed reverently as the hearse passed.

"That was a nice thing to do," remarked his mate.

"Well," said the Crewe fan, "She was a good wife to me for thirty odd years."

Four Chester University students taking their chemistry degree had done very well in their exams so far. Because of this, even though their last exam of the year was fast approaching, the four friends decided to go back to their hometown of Nantwich and catch up with some friends there. They had a great time partying.

However, after all the fun, they slept all day on Sunday and didn't make it back to Chester until early Monday morning which was the time of their final exam. Rather than taking the exam, they decided to find their professor after it was over and explain to him why they missed it. They told him that they had gone home to do some studying for the weekend and had planned to come back in time for the exam. But unfortunately, they had a flat tyre on the way back, didn't have a spare, and couldn't get help for a long time. As a result, they had only just arrived!

The professor thought it over and then agreed they could make up their final exam the following day. The four were very relieved. They studied hard that night - all night - and went in the next day at the time the professor had told them. He placed them in separate rooms and handed each of them a test booklet and told them to begin.

The first problem was worth five points. It was something simple about a specific chemistry topic. "Great," they all thought, "This is going to be easy." They each finished the problem and turned the page. On the second page was written, "Question 2 (for 95 points): Which tyre?"

Derek and Duncan were long-time neighbours in Knutsford. Every time, Derek saw Duncan coming round to his house, his heart sank. This was because he knew that, as always, Duncan would be visiting him in order to borrow something and he was fed up with it.

"I'm not going to let Duncan get away with it this time," he said quietly to his wife, "Watch what I'm about to do."

"Hi there, I wondered if you were thinking about using your hedge trimmer this afternoon?" asked Duncan.

"Oh, I'm very sorry," said Derek, trying to look apologetic, "but I'm actually going to be using it all afternoon."

"In that case," replied Duncan with a big grin, "You won't be using your golf clubs, will you? Mind if I borrow them?"

There's a man in Stoke-on-Trent who claims to have invented a game that's a bit like cricket; what he doesn't realise is Staffordshire County Cricket Club's been playing it for years.

Psychiatrist: "What's your problem?"

Patient: "I think I'm a chicken."

Psychiatrist: "How long has this been going on?"

Patient: "Ever since I was an egg!"

Two Alvanley Cricket Club players are chatting in the bar after a match. "So did you have a hard time explaining last week's game to the wife?" says one.

"I certainly did, "says the other," She found out I wasn't there!"

Three Cheshire women are talking in a bar about a party they've been invited to.

The first one says,"We've got to all wear an item that matches something belonging to our husbands at this party, haven't we?"

"Yeah," said the other two,"But what?"

The first one continued,"Well, my husband's got black hair and I've got a little black dress I can diet into by then."

The second one says,"That's a good idea. My husband has got brown hair and I've got a brown dress I can diet into by then too."

The third one looks a bit hesitant and says,"I just need to go on a diet - my husband's bald!"

"Dad," says the little boy,"Can I play football with the lads in the street?"

"No," says his dad,"They swear too much."

"But you play with them, Dad?"

"I swear already."

Darren proudly drove his new convertible into Runcorn and parked it on the main street. He was on his way to the recycling centre to get rid of an unwanted gift, a foot spa, which he left on the back seat.

He had walked half way down the street when he realised that he had left the top down with the foot spa still in the back.

He ran all the way back to his car, but it was too late...another five foot spas had been dumped in the car.

Q: What do you call a Staffordshire bloke in the 4th Round of the FA Cup?

A: The Referee.

Q: What's the difference between Stoke City and a teabag?

A: A teabag stays in the cup a lot longer.

Ten women out on a hen night in Widnes thought it would be sensible if one of them stayed more sober than the other nine and looked after the money to pay for their drinks. After deciding who would hold the money, they all put twenty pounds into the kitty to cover expenses. At closing time after a few beers, several vodka and cokes, and a Pina Colada each, they stood around deciding how to divvy up the leftover cash.

"How do we stand?" said Sharon.

"Stand?!" said Debbie. "That's the easy part! I'm wondering how I can walk. I've missed the last bus to Appleton!"

A lawyer at Chester Crown Court says to the judge, "Your Honour, I wish to appeal my client's case on the basis of newly discovered evidence."

His Lordship replies, "And what is the nature of the new evidence?"

The lawyer says, "My Lord, I discovered that my client still has £500 left."

A man rushed into Halton General Hospital and asked a nurse for a cure for hiccups. Grabbing a cup of water, the nurse quickly splashed it into the man's face.

"What did you that for?" screamed the man, wiping his face. "Well, you don't have the hiccups now, do you?" said the nurse.

"No," replied the man. "But my wife out in the car does.

One afternoon at Chester University, a group of freshers, who had just started their psychology course, were attending one of their first seminars. The topic was emotional extremes.

"Let's begin by discussing some contrasts," said the tutor. He pointed to a student in the front row, "What is the opposite of joy?"

The student thought about it briefly, then answered "Sadness". The tutor asked another student, "What is the opposite of depression?"

She paused then said, "Elation."

"And you," the tutor said to another student sitting at the back, "What about the opposite of woe?"

The student thought for a moment, then replied, "Um, I believe that would be 'giddy up'."

For a minute Port Vale were in with a chance - then the game started.

Albert, an extremely wealthy 65 year-old, arrives at Old Hall Country Club with a beautiful 25-year-old blonde on his arm. His buddies at the club are all aghast. They corner him and ask, "Albert, how did you get the trophy girlfriend?"

"Girlfriend!" exclaims, Albert, "She's my wife!"
His friends are shocked, but continue to ask, "So, how'd you persuade her to marry you?"

Albert replies, "I lied about my age."

His friends respond, "What do you mean? Did you tell her you were only 50?"

Albert smiles and says, "No, I told her I was 81."

In the staff canteen, Jim was always showing Bob photos of his dog and saying how clever it was: doing tricks, playing ball, bringing his newspaper and slippers. One day Jim brought in the album from his daughter's wedding so Bob could look through the photos. Bob decided to tease Jim a little and said, "Hang on, where`s your precious dog? I'm surprised he wasn't the Best Man!"

Jim looked at Bob as if he was stupid, "Don't be silly, someone had to take the photos"

A woman walked into the kitchen to find her husband stalking around with a fly swatter. "What are you doing?" She demanded.

"Hunting flies," he replied.

"Oh. Killed any?" She asked.

"Yep, three males and two females," he replied.

Intrigued, she said, "How can you tell?"

"Three were on a beer can, and two were on the phone," he replied.

Q: Why was the sheep arrested on the M6?

A: She did a ewe-turn

Q: What has eight legs, four ears and twice as much wool as the average sheep?

A: Two sheep

In a school in Runcorn, a little boy just wasn't getting good marks. One day, his teacher was checking his homework and said, "Lee, once again I'm afraid I can only give you two out of ten."

Little Lee looked up at her and said, "Well, Miss, I don't want to scare you, but…"

He stopped, a worried expression on his face.

"What is it? Tell me, Lee," said his teacher kindly.

"Well," said the boy, "my daddy says if I don't get better marks soon, somebody is going to get a spanking."

A police officer arrived at the scene of a major pile up on the A41.

The officer runs over to the front car and asks the driver, "Are you seriously hurt?"

The driver turns to the officer and says, "How should I know? Do I look like a lawyer?"

A man walks into a bank in Altrincham and says to the female assistant at the counter, "I want to open a credit account now!"

To which the lady replied,"I beg your pardon, sir, what did you say?"

"Listen cloth-ears," snapped the man aggressively, "I said I want to open a credit account right now."

"Sir, I'm sorry but we do not tolerate rudeness to staff in this bank!"

The clerk left the window and went over to the bank manager and complained to him about her customer. They both returned and the manager asked,"What seems to be the problem here?"

"There's no problem," the man said, "I just won 50 million in the lottery and I want to open a credit account in this bank right now!"

"I see, sir," the manager said, "and this silly woman is giving you a hard time?"

At The Bird in Hand in Guilden Sutton, a newcomer asked an elderly local regular, "Have you lived here all your life?"

The old man took a sip of his ale and, after a long pause, replied, "Don't know yet!"

An old bloke at the bus stop outside The Countess of Chester Hospital is talking to the next person in the queue whilst rubbing his head.

"My wooden leg ain't half giving me some gyp," complained the old boy.

The person in the queue looks at him, wondering why he keeps rubbing his head, and says, "Really? Why?"

The old man retorted, "Cos my missus keeps hitting me over the head with it!"

A policeman stops a man in a car in the middle of Chester with a sheep in the front seat.

"Ah do, what are you doing with that sheep?" He asks. "You should take it to a zoo."

The following week, the same policeman sees the same man again with the sheep in the front seat of the car. Both of them are wearing sunglasses. The policeman pulls him over. "I thought you were going to take that sheep to the zoo?"

The man replies, "I did. We had such a good time we are going to the beach this weekend!"

Sam worked in a telephone marketing company in Warrington. One day he walked into his boss's office and said, "I'll be honest with you, I know the economy isn't great, but I have three companies after me, and, with respect, I would like to ask for a pay rise."

After a few minutes of haggling, his manager finally agreed to a 5% pay rise, and Sam happily got up to leave.

"By the way," asked the boss as Sam went to the door, "Which three companies are after you?"

"The electric company, the water company, and the phone company," Sam replied.

A farmer was driving along a country road near the village of Northwich with a large load of fertiliser. A little boy, playing in front of his house, saw him and called out, "What do you have on your truck?"

"Fertiliser," the farmer replied.

"What are you going to do with it?" asked the little boy. "Put it on strawberries," answered the farmer.

"You ought to live here," the little boy advised him. "We put sugar and cream on ours."

FERTILISER
FERTILISE
FERTILISE

It was a quiet night in Winsford and a man and his wife were fast asleep, when there was an unexpected knock on the door. The man looked at his alarm clock. It was half past three in the morning. "I'm not getting out of bed at this time," he thought and rolled over.

There was another louder knock.

"Aren't you going to answer that?" asked his wife irritably.

So the man dragged himself out of bed and went downstairs. He opened the door to find a strange man standing outside. It didn't take the homeowner long to realise the man was totally drunk.

"Hi there," slurred the stranger. "Can you give me a push?" "No, I'm sorry I most certainly can't. It's half past three in the morning and I was in bed," said the man and he slammed the front door.

He went back up to bed and told his wife what happened. "That wasn't very nice of you," she said. "Remember that night we broke down in the pouring rain on the way to pick the kids up from the babysitter, and you had to knock on that man's door to get us started again? What would have happened if he'd told us to get lost?" "But the man who just knocked on our door was drunk,"

replied her husband.

"Well, we can at least help move his car somewhere safe and sort him out a taxi," said his wife. "He needs our help."

So the husband got out of bed again, got dressed, and went downstairs. He opened the door, but couldn't to see the stranger anywhere so he shouted, "Hey, do you still want a push?"

In answer, he heard a voice call out, "Yes please!"

So, still unable to see the stranger, he shouted, "Where are you?"

"I'm over here, mate," the stranger replied, "on your swing."

Everyday a lady walks past a pet shop in Warrington on her way to work. One day she notices a parrot in the window and stops to admire the bird. The parrot says to her, "Ah do, old duck, you've got a right ugly mug."

Well, the lady is furious! She storms off but on her way back from work she passes the same parrot and, when it sees her, the bird says, "Ah do, old duck, you've got a right ugly mug."

She is incredibly angry now so she goes to the manager and threatens to sue the pet shop. She demands to have the bird put down. The manager apologises profusely and promises that the bird won't say it again. The next day, she walks past the parrot and, when it sees her, it says, "Ah do, old duck."

The woman stops, scowls and with an icy stare, says, "Yes?"

The parrot struts back and forth on its perch in a cocky manner, gawping at her, then it says, "You know."

The president of the Winsford Vegetarian Society really couldn't control himself any more. He simply had to try some pork, just to see what it tasted like. So one day he told his members he was going away for a short break. He left town and headed to a restaurant in Chester. He sat down, ordered a roasted pig, and waited impatiently for his treat. After only a few minutes, he heard someone call his name, and, to his horror, he saw one of his members walking towards him. At exactly the same moment, the waiter arrived at his table, with a huge platter, holding a whole roasted pig with an apple in its mouth. "Isn't this place something?" said the president, thinking quickly, "Look at the way they serve apples!"

Phil's nephew came to him with a problem. "I have my choice of two women," he said, with a worried frown, "A beautiful, penniless young girl whom I love dearly, and a rich widow who I don't really love."

"Follow your heart," Phil counselled, "marry the girl you love." "Very well, Uncle Phil," said the nephew, "That's sound advice. Thank you."

"You're welcome," replied Phil with a smile, "By the way, where does the widow live?"

A high-rise building was going up in Widnes, and three steel erectors sat on a girder having their lunch.

"Oh, no, not cheese and pickle again," said Jim, the first one, "If I get the same again tomorrow, I'll jump off the girder.'

Horace opened his packet. "Oh, no, not a chicken salad with lettuce and mayo," he said. "If I get the same again tomorrow, I'll jump off too."

Andy, the third man, opened his lunch. "Oh, no, not another potato sandwich," he said. "If I get the same again tomorrow, I'll follow you two off the girder."

The next day, Jim got cheese and pickle. Without delay, he jumped. Horace saw he had chicken salad with lettuce and mayo, and, with a wild cry, he leapt too. Then the third man, Andy, opened his lunchbox. "Oh, no," he said. "Potato sandwiches." And he too jumped.

The foreman, who had overheard their conversation, reported what had happened, and the funerals were held together.

"If only I'd known," sobbed Jim's wife.

"If only he'd said," wailed Horace's wife.

"I don't understand it at all," said Andy's wife. "He always got his own sandwiches ready."

A farmer from the Staffordshire once visited a farmer based near Malpas. The visitor asked, "How big is your farm?" to which the Cheshire farmer replied, "Can you see those trees over there? That's the boundary of my farmland".

"Is that all?" said the Staffordshire farmer, "It takes me three days to drive to the boundary of my farm."

The Malpas man looked at him and said, "I had a car like that once."

The nervous young batsman playing for Nantwich C.C. was having a very bad day. In a quiet moment in the game, he muttered to the one of his team mates, "Well, I suppose you've seen worse players."

There was no response...so he said it again, "I said 'I guess you've seen worse players'."

His team mate looked at him and answered, "I heard you the first time. I was just trying to think..."

One day at Victoria Infirmary in Northwich, a group of primary school children were being given a tour. A nurse showed them the x-ray machines and asked them if they had ever had broke a bone.

One little boy raised his hand, "I did!"

"Did it hurt?" the nurse asked.

"No!" he replied.

"Wow, you must be a very brave boy!" said the nurse. "What did you break?"

"My sister's arm!"

A Macclesfield woman called Mandy was still not married at thirty-five and she was getting really tired of going to family weddings especially because her old Aunt Maud always came over and said, "You're next!"

It made Mandy so annoyed she racked her brains to figure out how to get Aunt Maud to stop. Sadly, an old uncle died and there was a big family funeral. Mandy spotted Aunt Maud in the crematorium, walked over, pointed at the coffin and said, with a big smile, "You're next!"

At a school in Congleton, the maths teacher poses a question to little Wayne, "If I give £500 to your dad on 12% interest per annum, what will I get back after two years."

"Nowt," says Wayne.

"I am afraid you know nothing about maths, Wayne," says the teacher crossly.

"I am afraid too, sir," replies Wayne, "You know nowt about my father."

A man and his wife walked past a swanky new restaurant in Sandbach. "Did you smell that food?" the woman asked. "Wonderful!"

Being the kind-hearted, generous man that he was, her husband thought, "What the heck, I'll treat her!" So they walked past it a second time.

Peter walked up to the sales lady in the clothing department of Primark in Cheshire oaks.

"I would like to buy my wife a pretty pair of tights," he said. "Something cute with love-hearts or flower patterns."

"Oh, that's so sweet," exclaimed the sales lady, "I'll bet she'll be really surprised." "I'll say," said Peter, "she's expecting a new diamond ring!"

An expectant father rang the Macclesfield General Maternity Unit to see how his wife, who had gone into labour, was getting on. By mistake, he was connected to the county cricket ground.

"How's it going?" he asked.

"Fine," came the answer, "We've got three out and hope to have the rest out before lunch. The last one was a duck."

In the early days of television sets the ritual of switching the TV on and waiting for the valves to warm up was all part of building the excitement to watch a programme: usually the one that was on! In Poynton, an old miner, Jimmy Hubbard decided to tell his neighbour about his newly-acquired television and how he was going to watch the Queen's Coronation."I've gorra goo in now ter watch the spectacle," he said, looking at his pocket watch.

His neighbour looked and said,"But it in't on fer another three hours."

"I know," said Jimmy,"but they'n sayin' there'll be a lot there and I wants ter get a good seat!"

Did you hear about the last wish of the henpecked husband of a house-proud wife?

He asked to have his ashes scattered on the carpet.

A pupil at a school in Ellesmere Port asked his teacher, "Are 'trousers' singular or plural?"

The teacher replied, "They're singular on top and plural on the bottom.

A golfer was going around the Mollington Grange Golf Club course. He was talking to his caddy between holes about a forthcoming competition. "I've been drawn against Jack Smith from Alsager, is he any good?"

The caddy checked for a moment and said, "He's absolutely rubbish. Can't get around the course with any ease. He set a new course record for the worst round ever that has only just been beaten."

"Oh, I should easily get through to the next round then, shan't I?" said the golfer complacently.

The caddy looked down at the scorecard and said, "I wouldn't bet on it!"

Pete and Larry hadn't seen each other in many years. They were having a long chat, telling each other all about their lives. Finally Pete invited Larry to visit him in his new flat in Crewe. "I have a wife and three kids and I'd love to have you visit us."

"Great. Where do you live?"

"Here's the address. There's plenty of parking behind the flat. Park and come around to the front door, kick it open with your foot, go to the lift and press the button with your left elbow, then enter! When you reach the sixth floor, go down the hall until you see my name on the door. Then press the doorbell with your right elbow and I'll let you in."

"Great. But tell me...what is all this business of kicking the front door open, then pressing elevator buttons with my right, then my left elbow?"

Pete answered, "Surely you're not coming empty-handed?"

A Hurrah Henry from Lichfield was driving around Runcorn in his fancy new BMW and realised that he was lost. The driver stopped a local character, old Tom, and said, "Hey, you there! Old man, what happens if I turn left here?"

"Dunna know sir," replied Tom.

"Well, what if I turn right here - where will that take me?" continued the visitor.

"Dunna know, sir," replied old Tom.

Becoming exasperated, the driver continued, "Well, what if I go straight on?"

A flicker of knowledge passed over old Tom's face but then he replied, "Dunna know, sir."

"I say, old man, you don't know a lot do you?" retorted the posh bloke.

Old Tom looked at him and said, "I may not know a lot, sir, but I ain't lost like what you are!" With that, old Tom walked off leaving the motorist stranded.

POSH 1